MY CHILDHOOD INSPIRATIONS
BOOK 3: School Daze

by Joyce Green

MY CHILDHOOD INSPIRATIONS
BOOK 3: School Daze

Joyce Green

Copyright © 2022 by Joyce Green

All rights reserved. This book or any portion thereof may not be reproduced or used in any manner whatsoever without the express written permission of the author and/or publisher except for the use of brief quotations in a book review.

Edited by: Anthony Ambrogio

Illustrators: Kat Powell ("That Dog")
  Kat Powell ("My First School Play")
  Vox Illustration ("I'm a Snowbird")
  Eric Muchira ("Jump Rope")
  Kat Powell ("The Sewing Basket")

Publisher: G Publishing LLC

ISBN: 978-0-9969684-4-7

Library of Congress Control Number: 2015920431

Published and Printed in the United States of America

Warm Acknowledgements to my
Grandchildren for Ideas and Insights!

Sequoyeth Simpson
Sheyenne Simpson
Shaydon Simpson

I wrote these true stories for my grandchildren

Table of Contents

That Dog 9
My First School Play 19
"I'm a Snowbird." 27
Jump Rope! 37
Saturday at the Movies 45
The Sewing Basket 56

That Dog

"RUN! *RUUUUN!!!* That big mean dog is out!" shouted Stevie. Stevie was one of the boys who lived in the block. My friends and I, taking the long way home from school today, were busy talking and laughing together.

*****

We walked down the street where that big dog lived almost every day. Every time we walked past that big dog's house, the dog would come running up to the fence and growl and bark at us.

That fence kept the dog in his yard and from getting us. Still, that dog would jump on the fence at us. That dog tried to scare us. And he DID!!!

We were five, sometimes six, children who walked home together. Usually, when we knew we were about to pass "That Dog," we got ready for him to charge at us, knowing that he was probably lying in wait for us.

And, like clockwork, there he came, right at us, barking and growling. At first, we froze every time, even though the fence kept the dog in the yard.

After a while, we got used to that dog barking and growling at us. When he would come running to the gate to growl and bark at us, my friends and I would walk in the street and tell him to "Shut up, dog."

Some of the other children, especially the boys, would taunt the dog with sticks. They would pretend to growl and bark just like that dog, right back at the dog.

That dog got real mad and loud. He tried to jump the fence to get them. "*Oooh*," I warned, "you better leave that dog alone." But they kept picking at the dog.

*****

Today, when we heard Stevie's warning about the dog, we remembered what some of us had done to that dog. Now we were stuck in the middle of the block, and that dog could be anywhere.

"THERE'S THE DOG!" someone shouted.

We were terrified. That dog had his ears back and his tongue out. He looked like a lion ready to pounce on his food.

My friends and I were frozen where we were standing. Where could we go? What could we do? Suddenly the other children started screaming and running. One friend ran and tried to climb the fence at the dog's house.

I stood still and closed my eyes.

The next thing I knew, that dog was standing there smelling me

and my face. I wet my panties a little.

I kept my eyes closed real tight. I was sure that dog was going to eat me up.

But that dog turned and ran to my friend who was holding on to the fence. She started crying. He sniffed her. I think that dog wanted to get away from the fence gate. So he left her alone too.

The dog could hear the other children yelling. He saw some of them running through the empty lot across the street from his house.

The dog took off after them. He was like a little horse with ferocious teeth. His ears went back and he was growling.

Everybody split up, running in different directions. The dog looked around and decided to go after the closest ones to him. That was the twins.

Those girls were hollering for dear life. My friend and I ran to another friend's house. She lived two houses away from where I had been standing.

But the twins lived around the corner. The twins were screaming like they were getting a real hard beating. The dog was coming right at them. They made it to their home gate just in time, though.

That dog spun around looking for ... *who's next?*... The dog came running back towards his house. Then he saw the boys who had thrown rocks and jabbed sticks at him.

The dog went after them in a fury. He caught one boy's pants leg. He bit his pant and ripped a piece of cloth off.

The boy was screaming. Then the dog recognized another boy who had teased and taunted him. He took off after him.

The dog angrily grabbed the boy's shirt with his teeth. He growled, shaking his head back and forth, pulling that boy's shirt as hard as he could.

The dog put a big hole in that boy's shirt. The boy was screaming, "Help, help, he's gonna eat me!"

Then the dog saw a little girl walking through the lot next to the house I was hiding in.

The girl was about seven years old. The girl lived around the corner from the dog. She was new in the neighborhood. The dog turned, growling, and raced directly toward her.

We screamed at her from the screened front door, "Run, Run! That dog is going to bite you!" The girl just stood there trying to understand what we were saying to her. But the dog was already there.

The dog ran up to her and growled. She looked at the dog ...

The dog looked at her. She looked away and just kept on walking quietly. The dog barked a little, then wagged his tail. He turned around to find somebody else.

By now, the dog's owner had come home. He ran out of the house, yelling for the dog to come home.

The dog looked around a few more times and then ran to his owner. The owner fussed at the dog and put him back into the yard behind the fence.

My friend and I left our hiding place at my other friend's house. We were in a big hurry to get home. I wanted to get home just in case that dog got loose again.

I started running. I ran past that girl who stood there looking at the dog. She looked at me; I looked at her.

"Didn't that dog scare you?" I asked on the run.

She replied matter-of-factly, "No,". and walked home.

After that day, all the children in the neighborhood knew about the new girl. She was famous.

*****

From then on, some of the children stopped picking at that dog. But those boys still bothered the dog by kicking the fence where he was.

Every day we told those boys, "You better leave that dog alone!" But they didn't listen.

So the dog continued to bark and growl and try to get them. For a while he barked at me and my friend too.

After a while, he stopped and just looked at us when we walked by. I guess he got used to us and got bored. Or maybe he knew we were looking out for him by scolding those boys and appreciated it.

My First School Play

Daddy bought Ma a sewing machine. Ma used the sewing machine to make quilts, bedspreads, curtains, dresses, and blouses. When I started school, Ma made my dresses.

Where we lived, a lot of ladies had sewing machines. They made some of their own clothes. Ma made some of her own dresses too.

Ma used Simplicity, Mc-Call's, and, sometimes, Vogue patterns that she bought from Grants or H.L. Green, the 5&10 discount stores.

Sometimes Ma got fancy patterns from S. Klein Department Store.

Ma said that putting a pattern together with your own material was like fixing a puzzle. When you finished and it looked good, you felt like the greatest sewer in the neighborhood.

Ma probably *was* the greatest sewer in the neighborhood.

She could sew, farm, and cook better than most of the people in our whole neighborhood because she grew up on a farm.

When I was in the second grade, my class was going to put on a play. It was about the pilgrims, Indians, and Thanksgiving.

The majority of my classmates were White, just like the pilgrims. But, in the school play, I got to be a pilgrim too.

All the children's mothers were asked to make their children's outfits for the play. Ma made my outfit.

It was really beautiful. She made a pilgrim hat, blouse, and skirt.

Ma told me, "I used to thread needles for momma and the other ladies when they were quilting. I was real little."

"Momma, your momma had a quilting group?"

That's how I learned how to sew."
Momma would make teacakes and tea for the quilting ladies.

She taught me many different sewing stitches, like the drop stitch and the running stitch.

"I taught myself how to use the sewing machine. So I used the sewing machine and those stitches to make your outfit."

*****

On the day of the play, a lot of people came to our school. Most of them were parents. Ma came too. Ma always came to our activities at the school.

The play began. "Oh, we have landed in the New World," shouted three of my classmates who were on stage.

I came on stage with the next group of children. We were pilgrims. "We are on land!" we said. The second group, the group I was in, formed a double line on stage. I was in the back row.

I was so proud. My pilgrim outfit looked so much better than all of the other children's outfit, even if I was hidden in the second row.

The play lasted about 40 minutes, including the scenery changes. When the play was over, the audience clapped real loud.

The principal said something to the people. They clapped again, and it was over. Ma was waiting, and I ran to her when I saw her.

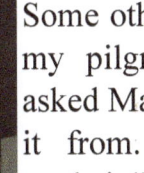

Some other parents saw my pilgrim outfit and asked Ma where she got it from. Ma said, "I made it." Their eyes got big, and their eyebrows went up on their foreheads. They looked real funny! Ma smiled as we left the gym.

*****

Still wearing my pilgrim outfit, I skipped alongside Ma as we walked home.

When we got one block away from home, Ma stopped to talk to Mrs. Fowler, a neighbor. Mrs. Fowler saw my pilgrim outfit and asked, "What do we have here?"

"I was in a play at school," I said, "and I was a pilgrim."

Mrs. Fowler laughed and said, "I bet you were the best-looking pilgrim in the play!" I curtsied and nodded.

"Ma, can I go home?"
"Yes," she said. "I'll be coming in a few minutes."

So I skipped down the street in my pilgrim outfit towards my house.

As I skipped down the street, I saw some of my friends on the block, playing. They saw me in my pilgrim outfit. They ran over to where I was and looked me up and down.

"Why you wearing those clothes and that hat?" one of them asked.

"I was in a play at school," I said, "and this is my costume!"

"What did you do in that play?" a boy asked.

"I was a pilgrim!" I said.

"A PILGRIM!!" they all shouted together.

"Uh huh," I nodded.

"But you're colored," said the boy. (Back then, Black people were called "colored people" or "coloreds.") "There ain't no colored pilgrims," he claimed.

"Yeah," said the girl, Paula, "I never seen no colored pilgrims either,"

I thought to myself for the first time that I never saw any colored pilgrims in my books either. "But," I said, "I was a pilgrim, and so was two other colored children."
"Were there Indians?"

Yes," I said.

"You shoulda been a Indian, like you momma," a boy said.

"The Indians came on the stage last," I said.

"Were they colored?" asked Paula.

"No," I said.

"You stupid," said the boy. And they all started laughing.

"I am not," I yelled.

I saw Ma coming down the street, and I ran home. When I got home, I waited for Ma on the porch. When Ma got there, she said, "Go change your clothes."

"Mommy," I asked her, "were there any colored pilgrims?"

Ma looked at me and said, "None I ever heard of."

"Then how come I was a pilgrim in the play?"

"Ask your teacher," Ma said.

I ran upstairs. I took off my pilgrim outfit. I put it on the bed and looked at it. It looked so nice.

I thought about what the children said about no colored pilgrims. (Of course, some of my White classmates who played pilgrims were Italian and Polish and Jewish. And there never were any Italian or Polish or Jewish pilgrims either. We were all pretending to be part of a group we never were part of because we were all Americans. But I didn't know that or think about that at the time.)

After I had changed clothes, I came downstairs. I thought about colored pilgrims again.

After that day, I never talked about the play or put that pilgrim outfit on again!

"I'm a Snowbird."

When I was in the third grade, and the school day was over, I used to take a shortcut home. (If I was with my friends, I would take the long way to get home.)

One cold snowy day, I was walking home from school with my friends, but—be-cause it was so cold and snowy—I decided to take the shortcut home to get there faster.

To take the shortcut, you had to cross a big long field, slide down the cement brook border, and run up the other side through a path in a lot to the street. The lot led to the street two blocks from my house.

I had taken the shortcut home many times before. But it was warm outside then, and there was no snow.

Today, it was snowing. The snow had been falling since last night. The big long field was covered with about a foot of snow.

When I started walking across the field, the snow was so high that it got all in my boots. It felt real cold. I kept going, though. Soon, I stopped walking and looked up at the sky.

Oooo! Snowflakes were falling all over my face. Even on my eyelashes. It tickled.

Maybe I'll make a snow angel, I thought. Everything around me was covered with snow, even the trees.

I was carrying a workbook. I set the book down on the snow. Then I plopped down on my butt in the snow. I lay down on my back in the snow.

I stretched my arms out like a "T." I stretched my legs out like an upside-down "V." I flapped my legs and arms back and forth like I was flying.

When I got up, snow went all down my neck and my back. I screamed because it was real cold and wet. I looked at the snow bird I made in the snow. It was beautiful.

I picked up my workbook. It was all wet from the snow. *Uh-oh, I'd better get home.*

I ran through the long field to where I thought the four big rocks were lined up in the water. That's where we would cross the brook.

The brook came from the drainage system of the water works. The brook was a long, narrow stream of water that ran through the big long field. It was sunk into the ground. There was a slanted cement wall on each side of the brook.

The brook flowed under the street. Sometimes, when it was warm, you could see different colors in the water in the brook. It looked like an oily rainbow.

Once in a while, when my brothers and I were running home from school to get lunch, we would take the shortcut across the rocks in the brook.

But, this day, the snow covered all the rocks. There was even snow on the cement that bordered the brook.

I could tell there were rocks in the water, so I thought that that's where I should cross the brook.

I slowly tried to ease down the slanted cement wall where the rocks were. The wet snow made the wall very slippery. So, I slid ... right down to-ward the water.

"*Yeow!*" I screamed. I tried to stop, but the cement was too slippery. My boots sank into the water and snow, and water got into my boots, again. I slid farther. The back of my dress got wet. So did my underpants. I was freezing!

I ran across the brook rocks, slipping off one of them back into that cold water again. Now I was frustrated and crying—especially since I couldn't get up the snow-covered cement border on the other side of the brook. There was nothing to grab on to. I kept slipping back into the water.

My work book was soaked. The cover came off. I was really crying now, and I was mad!

Finally, I found my balance and man-aged to climb up the cement border. I ran through the path to the street.

I was freezing and wet, and I had two blocks to go.

Cars were moving real slow on the snowy street. The snow was coming down real heavy now.

I was shivering as I ran down the street towards my house.

When I reached the back path to my house, I started crying again.

Ma was there, dressed in her coat and boots. She had been looking for me.

Ma yelled, "Where've you been? All the other children have been home for more than twenty minutes. I've been lookin' all over for you. Why are you all wet?"

Then I began crying real loud. Daddy came in the house. He had been looking for me too. "Where you been?" asked Daddy.

I tried to tell my story, but I was so cold and wet I could hardly talk. "Look at the back of your coat and dress," said Ma. "You're all wet and dirty!"

"*Waah!*" I cried with snot coming out my nose, "I fell in the water in the brook. I was taking the short-cut home, like my brothers do. I stopped and made a snowbird in Bradley Field."

I continued, "I slid down the cement wall into the water at the brook. I couldn't stop sliding. Snow and water got in my boots. The back of my dress and coat went into the water. My book is all wet, and the front came off."

Ma looked at Daddy. She grabbed me and pulled the wet clothes and boots off me. Daddy looked at her, then turned his head and smiled. I saw him do that.

I was sure I was in trouble, but they just got busy doing what they had been doing before I got home.

Ma made me take a hot bath, eat, and go to bed.

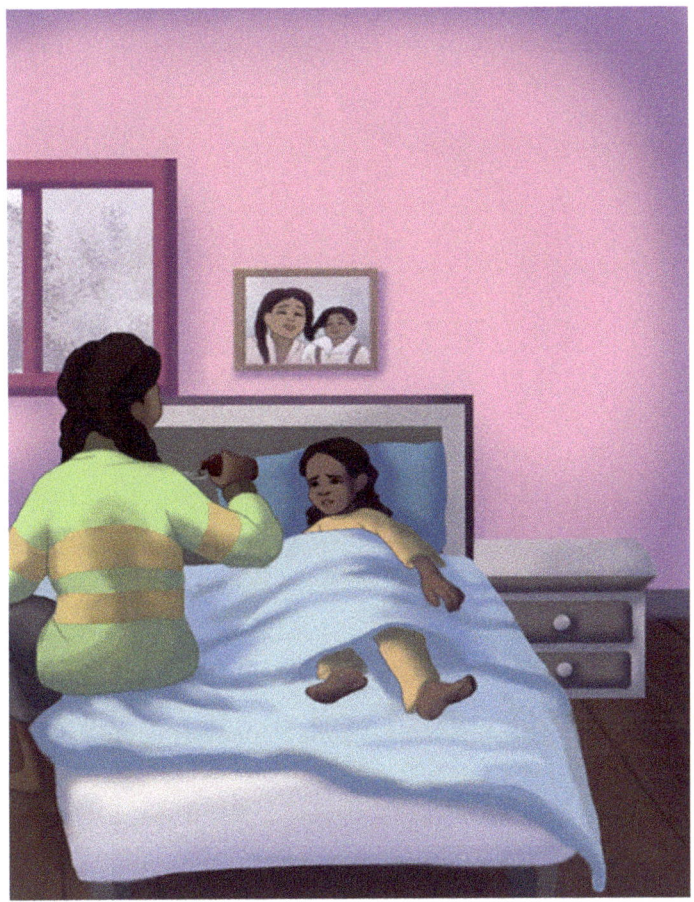

The next day I had to stay home from school. I was sneezing and blowing my nose a lot. I felt real hot, too.

Ma gave me some castor oil. It tasted real nasty. Ma said I had a fever. I stayed in bed for three days.

*****

Many years passed, and I did make other snowbirds in Bradley Field. I took the long way home, though. I always remembered that taking the long way home was the safest and best way.

I learned that, sometimes, shortcuts might get you where you need to go faster, but there may be some things, along the way, that might be more dangerous than taking the long, safe way.

Jump Rope!

One day after school, my friends and I were jumping rope in the street in front of my house.

There were four of us girls from the neighborhood arguing about who was supposed to jump first and who was supposed to turn the jump rope.

Finally, two girls started turning the jump rope, and the other two girls, one of whom was me, lined up to jump.

The two girls who were turning the rope were sisters. One of the sisters was big, and the other one was bigger.

Both sisters thought they were the queens of jumping and turning the jump rope.

For some reason, when it was my turn to jump, I would get stuck rocking back and forth, trying to get my timing right, to get in under the rope. I always messed up. The rope always caught me before I could get in under the rope safely.

Every time it was my turn to jump or turn the jump rope, the big girls would moan and make fun of me. They wanted me to know that they were better at jumping rope and turning the rope than me. They were.

Little did I know that the real reason they made fun of me was because they were jealous of me. I was slender and cute and, in their eyes, drew more friends and attention to myself than they drew to themselves.

Unknowingly, I still tried to learn how to jump rope and turn the rope so that I could be their friend.

That early fall afternoon, when those two big sisters were laughing at me trying to turn the jump rope, my Auntie May came down the street towards where we were playing. My Auntie May lived with us. She had just gotten back from running errands and saw how those big girls were treating me.

Auntie May, obviously annoyed, came over to where we were jumping rope. It was my turn to jump.

As usual, I got stuck trying to jump into the turning jump rope. I rocked back and forth so long that the rope turners would get mad. "Jump in," they would start yelling at me, "Jump in!" I'd try, but the rope would get in my way. When I tried to jump in fast, the rope would get tangled in my feet.

Auntie May placed the bag she was carrying on the grass near the sidewalk that led to the front door of my house and swiftly came over to where we were jumping rope, pushed me out of line, and took her place as "next."

Auntie May had on a white sleeveless blouse and kaki brown shorts that were about four inches above her knees. She wore a pair of brown loafer flats on her feet.

The surprised jump-rope turners looked at Auntie May and giggled. They continued to turn the jump rope, though.

All of a sudden, Aunt May began to rock back and forth, back and forth, as she stood to the side of one of the rope turners.

"Turn that rope up higher and get a little closer together" she said. After all, Auntie Mae was 5' 10" inches tall. The rope-turners' eyes got real big! ... So did mine.

"SHE'S GONNA JUMP!" shouted one of the rope– turners

"Make the rope higher" the other one said.

They did, and Auntie May did it! She jumped in. We all started screaming, "She's jumping; she's jumping; she's jumping!"

I felt that I had been saved. Auntie May jumped for about two long minutes, and then her feet got caught up in the jump rope.

Everybody was amazed. We thought she was too old to jump rope. After all, she was 26 years old!

Auntie May finished jumping and walked over to where I was standing. She stood next to me.

Auntie May told the rope turners to turn the rope. They did. Then Auntie May said to me, "Jump! Get in there." My heart felt as if it was pounding in my throat. "Don't be afraid of the rope; time it and get in there," said Auntie May as she glared at the two big sisters.

They turned the rope without saying a word. I gathered up all my strength, rocked back and forth, and jumped in.

I jumped in when the rope was coming down, so I got all tangled up. The rope-turners rolled their eyes and let out these deep loud sighs.

Auntie May stood there and looked at me. Then she said, "Try it again." I did, and I got in.

This time I was so stunned that I got in I just stood still instead of continuing to jump.

"Do it again," said Auntie May, "but keep jumping."

I tried it again and got in. I kept jumping for about a minute.

"Do it again," said Auntie May.

I began to rock, and this time I was feeling it. I jumped in, and I was in! I jumped for what seemed like a good long jump.

The rope-turners looked at me and said, "It's your time to turn." I said, "Okay."

Auntie May smiled and winked at me. "Check your timing 'cause now you're as good as everybody else," she said before going into the house.

I was really proud of myself for learning how to jump in when the big girls were turning rope. But I was especially proud of my Auntie May, who made me believe that I could do it.

I walked toward my house as the girls began to play double-dutch. The biggest girl was jumping as the two other girls turned the rope.

Saturday at the Movies

My brother loved sports. He played baseball, basketball, football, and handball. Many times, my brother played on championship basketball teams. Though my brother was looked at as being a little guy, he was a gifted athlete.

My brother, kneeling in row 1, second from left, holding the basketball.

Sometimes, when there weren't any games, my brother liked to meet his friends at the movies. Since there were seven children in our family, ten cents per child for movie money, plus money for snacks, was too much money for my parents to spare for each child.

It was the mid-1950s, and, at that time, empty big Schaffer and Rheingold beer bottles could be redeemed for five cents each at George's, a local corner grocery store. George would also accept smaller empty Schaffer and Rheingold bottles for two cents each per bottle.

My brother would get up early in the morning and go about four blocks to Brierley Field's lover's lane. Sometimes he would find beer bottles in the lover's lane parking area. My brother would gather up to six beer bottles and lug them home in a brown paper bag.

I was at home while my brother looked for beer bottles, but I wanted to go to the movies too. So I got dressed and checked around the neighborhood for empty Coca Cola, Pepsi Cola, and other soda bottles to redeem at George's corner store. The empty soda bottles were worth two cents each, too. I found four bottles in our neighborhood.

My brother turned his beer bottles and my soda bottles in to George's store. He got 30 cents for his beer bottles and eight cents for my four soda bottles.

Together we had enough money to go to the movies. and to buy Rasinettes for me and Goobers Peanuts for him.

On one particular Saturday, my brother went out the back door and pulled his homemade bicycle out of the garage.

*****

We lived on Long Island in New York then. The weather was real cold and snowy in the winter and hot with some rain in the summer. My mother cleaned white people's houses in the daytime during the week. One white lady gave Ma her son's rusty old bike that had been lying against the side of her house for almost a year.

The white lady said to Ma, "Harvey, (her oldest son) has outgrown his bicycle. It's been lying against the house for about a year. You can take it home if you want. It has a flat tire and is a little rusty, but it still works. Maybe one of your boys can fix it and clean it up."

The bike was green with bent rusty silver fenders. The fenders had big brown rust spots, and the bicycle chain, around the foot pedals of the bicycle, was very rusty too.

Ma always walked home from work. We lived about a mile away from the white lady's house. The old bike had a flat tire, but Ma took her time and rolled it home anyway. When Ma got home, she called to my brother, "Here, if you can fix it and clean it up, you'll have something to ride." Then she presented him with the bicycle. He'd never had any bike, so he was happy to get that beat-up old bicycle.

My brother cased the neighborhood, looking through fields and lots for old discarded bicycles. He found a good old bike tire on a small bent bike in a lot three blocks away from our house. He removed the front wheel and rolled it home. At home, he worked on his bike.

My brother removed the front fender. He removed the front flat tire off the green bike and replaced it with the front tire from the little bike that he'd found in the lot. The little tire was two-thirds the size of the back tire of the big bike.

*****

Back then, bicycles had fat rubber tires with rubber inner tubes in the tires. The back tire was big, and the front tire was little. *I can't sit on the handlebars of that bike*, I thought. I dare not say anything, though. My brother was already mad because we might be late for the movie matinee.

I looked at the bicycle. There was a greasy rotating bicycle chain connected to the bicycle pedals. The bicycle handlebars could be twisted up or downward. If he wanted to go fast, my brother would twist the handlebars down, raise his bicycle seat up, and lean over to speed real fast.

My brother was ready to go. "Come on," he said. "Sit on the handlebars." Terrified, I looked at the bicycle again. I climbed on the bike and sat in the middle of the handlebars facing forward. *Squeak ...urk* went the handlebars when the handlebars fell downward. I almost fell off the bike as my brother struggled to keep the bike from falling over.

I was pretty big to be sitting on the handle bars of that bike, but my brother was unusually strong. He straightened that bike up, pushed the bike forward with me on the handlebars, and jumped on the bicycle's seat. I yelled, "OOOOO!"

Off we went. The movie theatre was over a mile away, so it was going to be a long bumpy ride, especially since my brother was peddling fast to make the 1:00 matinee.

We had four theaters in our village and several 5-&10-cent stores, including H.L. Green and W.T. Grant. We even had a Robert Hall men's clothing store. We had a bank, savings bank, police station, library, telephone company, and district courthouse.

There were restaurants and retail shops in the village. R & G Men's shop was right across from the bank, and Nedicks was across from R & G.in the center of town.

Nedicks was the spot! They had the best hot dogs with an orange drink. If you went there, you would see all your friends

Hempstead Theatre, Hempstead, NY

and schoolmates shopping or hanging out in the village.
Three of the theaters had movies that we could go to, but one theater showed what was then called "adult" movies (which would now be called "X rated" movies).

My brother and I went to the cheapest movie, where most of his and my friends were. When we got there, I saw a few of my friends. I wanted to sit with them. My brother told me that I could, but I better not go anywhere else. Then he went to sit with his friends.

The movie lasted a few hours. My friends and I changed our seats because the kids behind us were so loud and noisy that we missed hearing the good parts.

When the movie was over, my brother was looking for me because it was time to go home. But I decided to stay with my friends and watch what we missed when we sat in the other seats, where the noisy kids were.

Little did I know that my brother thought I left the theater and went home with my friends. So he went home without me.

When he got home and I was missing, he got into so much trouble. Aunt May was at home, and she saw my brother walk in the door without me.

"Where is your sister?" Aunt May shouted.

Stunned, my brother said, "I thought she came home. I couldn't find her in the movies."

Aunt May was furious. Impulsively, she slapped my brother and scolded him big time. "You better go find her right away,"

she shouted! Tearfully, my brother jumped on his bicycle and rode his bike back to the movie theater, looking for me.

By now, back at the movies, I was getting scared. It was getting late, and my friends were going home. I went back to where I had been sitting when I first got to the movies. Around 15 minutes later, my brother came to my seat and found me.

My brother was furious with me. "Where were you? I told you to stay where I could find you! I got into big trouble because I thought you left the movies and were walking home with your friends!" he screamed at me.

"My friends and I went to the seats on the other side of the aisle," I tried to explain. "Those kids who were sitting behind us were so noisy we couldn't hear the movie."

"You should have stayed where I told you to sit," he said. "You got me in trouble, and Aunt May slapped me because I came home without you. I'm gonna tell Daddy what she did. She's not supposed to hit us!"

We left the movie theater right away. I got back on his bike and sat on the handlebars. The sun was beginning to set, and we rode home in silence.

My brother got in trouble again when we got home. He had to deal with Daddy. He told Daddy that Aunt May had slapped him because she thought he had left the movies and come home without me when actually he thought that *I* had left the movies and come home first, without him.

"What—Aunt May slapped you?" Daddy yelled. "Did she know what happened?"

"No, I tried to tell her but she wouldn't listen," my brother said. Daddy was beside himself with anger.

I felt real bad about my brother getting in so much trouble because of me. He really didn't do anything wrong! But he was responsible for me, and he left the movies without me.

"There's no excuse for his actions!" Aunt May said to Daddy.

But Daddy wouldn't hear of it. NO ONE was allowed to touch his children, especially physically. He told Aunt May, "There's no excuse for *your* actions. You've got to go! NOW!"

Angrily, Aunt May left and went to her other sister's house.

Daddy looked at my brother and nodded. My brother looked at Daddy and smiled.

I think that was the last time my brother and I went to the movies together....

The Sewing Basket

It was the third period on a chilly fall day. Time for my home-economics class. I dreaded the thought. We were two weeks into the class, and I was without the required sewing basket.

The sewing basket was to contain a small variety pack of sewing needles, a thimble, black and white spools of thread, buttons (four small, white two-hole buttons and four white four-hole buttons), a tape measure, and one-and-a-half yards of material.

Ma and Daddy didn't have the money to buy me a sewing basket and all the things that were supposed to go into the basket. They were focused on buying school clothes, putting food on the table, and trying to keep oil in the oil burner to heat the house.

I hesitated as I reached the classroom door. All the girls in the home-economics class had laid their yard of material out on the table in front of them. Then they positioned their needles, scissors, thimble, and thread next to their material. Most of the girls sat back in their chairs, waiting for the teacher's instructions.

As I peered through the window of the class door, the bell rang "RRRR I I I N N N G!!

"Oh, no," I groaned. "Now I'm late." I opened the door and walked into the classroom.

"Uh-oh, you're late," one white girl whispered as I walked by her. I looked at her and rolled my eyes.

Another white girl nodded her head and said, softly, "Yeah, you're in trouble." Then she put her head down and giggled. I hated both of them for that.

"You are late! Take your seat. Where is your sewing basket," yelled the home-economics teacher.

I sat down in my seat and lowered my head. "I don't have a sewing basket," I mumbled softly.

"WHAT DID YOU SAY?" yelled that terrible teacher. I was so embarrassed. Many of the white girls in the class were snickering.

"I said, 'I DON'T HAVE A SEWING BASKET!'" I yelled.

Well, now that teacher was furious because I'd shouted back at her. "You can take yourself right down to the principal's office, right NOW!! Get your things and go," she yelled.

Oh no, I thought. The principal was worse than the home-economics teacher. I knew I was in a lot of trouble now.

*****

It was 1955. I was in the fifth grade at Washington Street Elementary School. One of my classes was home economics. Back then, in elementary school, most girls took Home Economics while Shop was for the boys.

At that time, elementary school went from kindergarten to eighth grade. We all were in one big building, but the older grades were to the left of the entrance, and the younger grades were to the right.

In our home-economics class, we studied sewing. We learned stitches like the running stitch, the basting stitch, the slide stitch, and others.

In addition, we learned basic cooking: how to boil an egg and make hot cereal. We toasted bread and made biscuits.

In shop, the boys made ash trays and learned how to cut and shape wood using tools like hammers, pliers, screw- divers, and little saws. The boys really loved shop. They had an opportunity to use the tools to make things with their hands.

Washington Street School, my elementary school, was predominantly white. The principal of the school was an old white woman who drove a clean, fancy silver-gray Cadillac car to school every day. She wore her thin silver-white hair like white British men of the 1700s. They wore white hair wigs with big curls in them. They looked old and funny. So did she.

Our principal—I'll call her Ms. "C"—was really strict. Even though Washington School was a public elementary school, Ms. C and an eighth-grade teacher ran Washington School like it was an upper-level private school.

At this school, there were several rules in place.

For girls:
- Girls could wear dresses or skirts and blouses only.
- All girls' dresses & skirts' hemlines must be 13 inches to the ground (nothing above the knee).
- Girls played any sports activity (softball, kick-ball, handball, etc,) in their daily dresses.

Washington Street School

For boys:
- Boys could not wear jeans.
- Boys must wear belts or suspenders.

For both girls and boys:
- Children must absolutely use no foul language (including "liar" or "lying").

*****

On this particular day, when my home-ec teacher sent me to the principal's office, Ms. C was on the phone. She glanced up at me, clearly annoyed.

"Why are you here?" she asked. Well, like most of the students in the school, I was terrified. I stood there quietly. *"Why are you here?"* she repeated loudly.

"I don't have a sewing basket, and the home-ec teacher told me to go to the principal's office."

Where's the note she gave you?" she asked. The note was in my hand. I held it out, and she snatched it from me.

"It says here that you were unprepared without your sewing

basket and you were rude and shouted at her," Ms. C said.

I was trembling, but I softly said, "I asked Ma if she could get me a sewing basket 'cause I needed it for school. She said she would get it. That was over two weeks ago."

"Well, where is it, then?" asked Ms. C.

"I don't know," I said.

"Go to that corner and face the wall," she said. "Maybe, the next time, you'll remember to bring your sewing basket for class."

With tears in my eyes, I walked over to the corner next to the principal's door. Facing the wall with my head down, I cried, I stood there for about 40 minutes, a whole class period, softly crying. People kept coming into Ms. C's office looking at me with pity and disgust.

I knew that we didn't have the money to buy a sewing basket. We were lucky to get two to three meals a day sometimes. But what really hurt was that I was the fifth child of my family to attend this school. Ms. C knew our family's situation, and, in addition, my older sister had also had problems with the home-economics teachers.

Later that evening, I told Ma what had happened in school. She looked at me, clearly surprised. I told her how everyone in class had sewing baskets but me and how some of those white girls were snickering when I was told to go to the principal's office. Ma put her head down and was quiet.

The next week, Ma made sure I had a sewing basket, and she helped me catch up with the stitches I missed learning about in The next week, Ma made sure I had a sewing basket, and she helped me catch up with the stitches I missed learning about in class. I really got good at those sewing stiches. Ma taught me the running stich, the basting stich, the back stich, and how to hem skirts and things.

Soon, I was able to hem my brother's pants for pay.

"Hey, sis, how about hemming up my new pants?" he asked.

"Twenty-five cents!" I shouted!

"WHAT?" he yelled, "Twenty-five cents is too much." "Okay, ten cents a leg," I said.

"That's too much too," he said. "Ten cents a leg," I insisted. Finally he said, "Okay."

I was always charging my brothers ten cents a leg to hem their pants from Robert Hall. My brothers didn't like it, but they wanted to wear their new pants, so they had to pay the price.

After I hemmed my brother's pants, I took the pants to him and said, "Here. Where's my money?"

He snatched the pants, smiled and said, "I'll give it to you later."

I was furious. He laughed and walked away.

I yelled, "MA, MA, he cheated me. I hemmed his pants and he owes me 10 cents!" Ma ignored me. I never got paid.

Years later, I made some of my own clothes. Sewing helped me get through many days when I was without a lot of money. But I will always remember being punished in front of everybody in the principal's office for being without a sewing basket.

www.ingramcontent.com/pod-product-compliance
Lightning Source LLC
Chambersburg PA
CBHW040311050426
42450CB00019B/3462